While I Am Sleeping

Written by Malaika Rose Stanley

Illustrated by Rachael Saunders

Published by Pearson Education Limited, 80 Strand, London, WC2R 0RL.

www.pearsonschools.co.uk

Text © Pearson Education Limited 2016
Designed by Bigtop Design Ltd

Original illustrations © Pearson Education Limited
Illustrated by Rachael Saunders

First published in the USA by Pearson Education Inc, 2016
First published in the UK by Pearson Education Ltd, 2016

20 19 18 17 16
10 9 8 7 6 5 4 3 2 1

British Library Cataloguing in Publication Data
A catalogue record for this book is available from the British Library

ISBN 978 0 435 16479 9

Printed in the UK by Ashford Colour Press

While I am sleeping and
tucked in my bed,
at night-time some people
are working instead.

3

The bakers make bread, chocolate cookies and pies

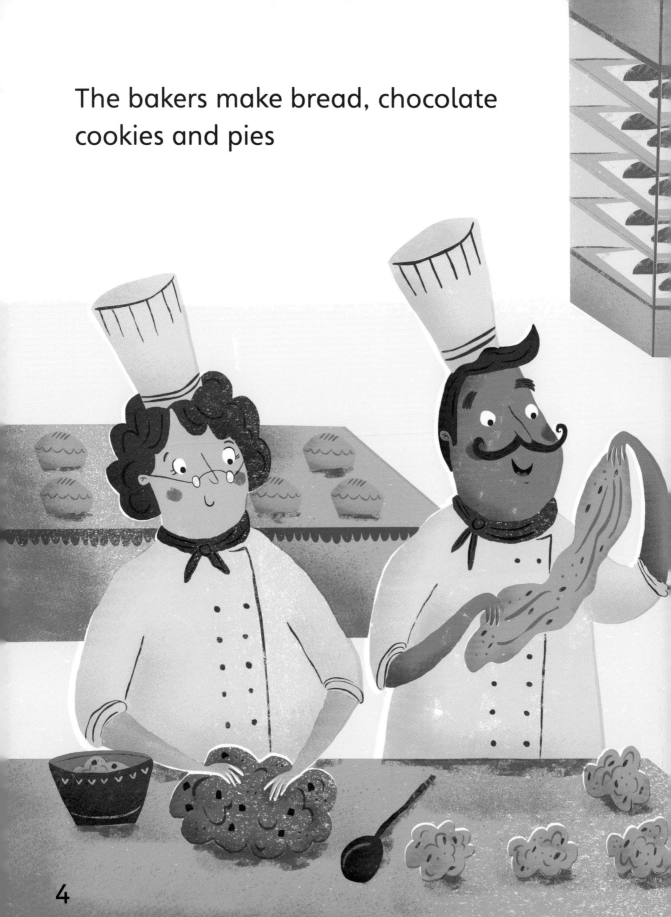

and gingerbread people with buttons and eyes.

While I am sleeping and tucked
in my bed,
at night-time some people are
working instead.

The garage assistant sells petrol
and oil,
soft drinks and coffee and snacks
wrapped in foil.

While I am sleeping and
tucked in my bed,
at night-time some people
are working instead.

Brave fire-fighters put out
hot flames with a hose,
and doctors take care of
sick patients who doze.

While I am sleeping and tucked
in my bed,
at night-time some people are
working instead.

Street cleaners sweep
pavements and empty the bins
of litter and gum and
banana skins.

While I am sleeping and tucked in my bed,
at night-time some people are working instead.

Ambulance drivers with sirens and lights
race to help people all through the night.

While I am sleeping and tucked
in my bed,
at night-time some people are
working instead.

Delivery drivers in lorries
and vans
drop off papers and food in
packets and cans.

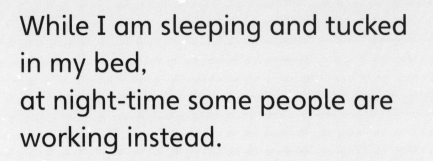

While I am sleeping and tucked
in my bed,
at night-time some people are
working instead.

When they are tired and need
a quick break,
they run to the café for coffee
and cake.

While I am sleeping and
tucked in my bed,
at night-time some
people are working
instead.

Market stallholders sell
fish and fresh meat,
and boxes of fruit that
taste oh-so-sweet.

While I am sleeping and tucked in my bed,
at night-time some people are working instead.

Supermarket workers fill up the shelves,
all laughing and joking amongst themselves.

While I am sleeping and tucked
in my bed,
at night-time some people are
working instead.

At stations and airports,
taxis wait in a row,
and the drivers take people
where they want to go.

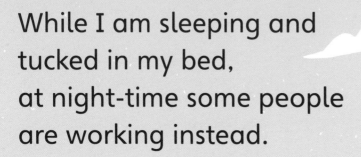

While I am sleeping and tucked in my bed, at night-time some people are working instead.

But when I wake up, bright and early each day, the night workers are snoozing and snoring away.